BIG
BIG TRUCKS

by Catherine Ipcizade

Consulting Editor: Gail Saunders-Smith, PhD

Consultant: Norb Marx
Branch Manager
Interstate Motor Trucks Inc.
Rochester, Minnesota

Capstone
press®

Mankato, Minnesota

Pebble Plus is published by Capstone Press,
151 Good Counsel Drive, P.O. Box 669, Mankato, Minnesota 56002.
www.capstonepress.com

 Books published by Capstone Press are manufactured with paper
containing at least 10 percent post-consumer waste.

Library of Congress Cataloging-in-Publication Data
Ipcizade, Catherine.
    Big trucks / by Catherine Ipcizade.
    p. cm. — (Pebble plus. Big)
    Includes bibliographical references and index.
    Summary: "Simple text and photographs present big trucks" — Provided by publisher.
    ISBN 978-1-4296-3314-7 (library binding)
    1. Trucks — Juvenile literature. I. Title. II. Series.
TL230.15.I67 2010
629.224 — dc22   2009001617

Editorial Credits
Erika L. Shores, editor; Ted Williams, designer; Jo Miller, media researcher

Photo Credits
Alamy/Glyn Thomas Photography, cover
Capstone Press/Karon Dubke, 5, 13, 15
Getty Images Inc./Dorling Kindersley, 21; Photographer's Choice/Bob Pool, 19; Tim Boyle, 17
PhotoEdit Inc./Dennis MacDonald, 7
Shutterstock/Betacam-SP, cover (tires); javarman, cover (background); Michael Stokes, 9; Robert Pernell, 11;
    Vera Handojo, 1

Note to Parents and Teachers

The Big set supports national science standards related to science, technology, and society.
This book describes and illustrates big trucks. The images support early readers in
understanding the text. The repetition of words and phrases helps early readers learn new
words. This book also introduces early readers to subject-specific vocabulary words, which are
defined in the Glossary section. Early readers may need assistance to read some words and to
use the Table of Contents, Glossary, Read More, Internet Sites, and Index sections of the book.

Table of Contents

Big

Engines roar. Tires turn.
Big trucks have big parts
for all kinds of work.

Semitrucks can be up to
65 feet (20 meters) long.

A broken car sits

on a tow truck's big flatbed.

Tow trucks take cars

to repair shops.

Size:

A tow truck's flatbed is usually
21 feet (6 meters) long.

Everything is big

on monster trucks.

The tires are 66 inches

(168 centimeters) tall.

Size:

Monster trucks can be
up to 12 feet (3.7 meters) tall.

Bigger

A concrete mixer's big drum
spins around.
Inside the drum, sand and
water mix to make concrete.

Size:

Concrete mixers can be
34 feet (10 meters) long.

A garbage truck can have
an 8-foot (2-meter) arm.
The big arm dumps out
garbage cans into the truck.

Size:

Garbage trucks can be
34 feet (10 meters) long.

CAUTION
WIDE
RIGHT
TURNS
DO NOT PASS
ON RIGHT

WM.
WASTE MANAGEMENT
(507) 388-1157
800-422-5785
www.wm.com

WM.
WASTE MANAGEMENT

Biggest

Fire trucks carry big ladders.
The ladder raises a firefighter
100 feet (30 meters)
into the air.

Size:

Fire trucks can be up to
50 feet (15 meters) long.

15

Tanker trucks bring gasoline
to service stations.
The big tank holds enough
gasoline to fill 600 cars.

Size:
Tanker trucks can be
60 feet (18 meters) long.

Logging trucks take
logs to mills.
The truck's big engine
helps pull the heavy load.

Size:

Logging trucks can be
65 feet (20 meters) long.

Some dump trucks are huge.

Controls in the cab

raise the big box.

Rocks and dirt spill out.

Size:

Some dump trucks have boxes
that hold up to 150 tons
(136 metric tons).

21

Glossary

arm — a piece of equipment attached to a garbage truck that the driver controls; the driver uses the arm to pick up garbage cans and dump the trash into the truck.

cab — an area for a driver to sit in a large truck or machine

control — a lever or switch used to make something work

drum — a turning container that mixes concrete

engine — a machine that makes the power needed to move something

flatbed — a long, flat trailer used to carry a heavy load

mill — a building with machines for turning wood, grain, or other materials into products

repair — to make something work again

tank — a large container that holds liquid

Read More

Bender, Lionel. *Trucks and Trailers.* On the Move. North Mankato, Minn.: Chrysalis Education, 2006.

Oxlade, Chris. *Trucks.* Transportation Around the World. Chicago: Heinemann, 2008.

Internet Sites

FactHound offers a safe, fun way to find Internet sites related to this book. All of the sites on FactHound have been researched by our staff.

Here's all you do:

Visit *www.facthound.com*

FactHound will fetch the best sites for you!

Index

Word Count: 148

Grade: 1

Early-Intervention Level: 18